Roberto Clemente

Constance Turner
Illustrated by Robert Castilla

Contents

Rigby®

The Young Roberto

Melchor and Luisa Clemente lived in Carolina, Puerto Rico. Luisa washed clothes for a living, and Melchor worked in the sugarcane fields. On August 18, 1934, a new baby boy was born to the loving family. They named their son Roberto.

Roberto grew up in Puerto Rico.

When Roberto was young, his father taught him to work hard for anything he really wanted just like his father worked hard in the fields. Sometimes he worked with his father in the fields. Roberto worked as hard as he could in school, but playing baseball was Roberto's favorite thing to do.

Roberto liked to throw rubber balls at the ceiling and walls of his bedroom. He learned that squeezing the balls, created from crushed paper or tightly wrapped socks, made his hands strong. To play baseball, he used other homemade things, such as a bat made from a tree branch.

Roberto practiced with whatever he could find.

Baseball was important to Roberto.

Roberto began playing on softball teams when he was eight years old. As a teen, he joined a baseball league, which is a group of teams that play against each other. Roberto was also on his high school baseball and track teams. Many people thought he would go on to run in the 1952 Olympic Games, but Roberto wanted to become a baseball player.

Going to Canada

Roberto played for a winter-league team in Puerto Rico called the *Cangrejeros,* or Crabbers, until he finished high school. He tried out for the Brooklyn Dodgers, a major-league baseball team in New York. Roberto and 71 other men tried out, but the Dodgers wanted only Roberto. The Dodgers sent Roberto to Canada where he played for the Dodgers' minor-league team called the Montreal Royals.

It was difficult for Roberto in Canada. Most people spoke either English or French, but Roberto spoke Spanish. He had to learn how to speak English so that he could do basic things, such as order food in a restaurant or ride a bus.

Ballpark Menu in the 1950s

Hotdog . . . . . . 15¢
Soda . . . . 10¢
Peanuts . . . . . 10¢
Popcorn . . . . . 10¢
Ice cream . . . . 10¢

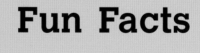

Fun Facts

- Major-league teams are the teams with the best players.
- Minor-league teams are made up of players who are training for the major leagues.

Another difficult thing for Roberto was that he hardly ever played when he was on the Montreal Royals. The Royals didn't want any other team to see how well Roberto played because then they would want him to be on their team.

Roberto played with the Montreal Royals for only one year.

Roberto was so upset about not playing that he thought about giving up baseball in Canada and going home to Puerto Rico. But then a man who worked for the Pittsburgh Pirates team told Roberto that he could play on the major-league Pirates team next year. But if he wanted to play the following year, he had to finish the season with the Royals. Roberto had some decisions to make.

Hard Work and Rewards

Roberto didn't give up. He kept playing baseball, moved from Canada to Pittsburgh, and became a baseball player for the Pirates in 1954. The first time he went up to bat in the major leagues, Roberto got a hit against his old team, the Dodgers! His powerful hitting skills and quick running speed helped him to play well.

Roberto was always ready to hit.

During his first year with the Pirates, Roberto had 121 hits out of the 474 times he was at bat. That means that he got a hit just about 1 out of every 4 times he came to bat. This is about 1/4 of the time, or 25%. He was hitting very well.

Roberto got 1 hit out of every 4 times he was at bat.

Roberto found that he had some of the same problems that he had faced in Canada. Roberto could speak English, but not very well. The language and way of life in Pittsburgh were very different from what he knew in Puerto Rico.

Even though life was difficult for Roberto, he always kept trying. In 1958 he tied a major-league record by hitting 3 triples in 1 game. A triple means that he ran all the way to third base after he hit the ball. His skills in the outfield earned him his first of 12 Golden Glove awards. He was also voted to play in the All-Star Game with the very best players in the major leagues.

Roberto and two of his teamates played in the All-Star Game.

Roberto's Fans

Roberto did everything he could to make baseball fun for the fans in the United States. He jumped high in the air and even crashed into fences to catch fly balls. He hit as hard as he could and always ran around the bases as fast as he could.

Roberto wanted to play a good game for his fans.

Roberto's family gathered with fans for Roberto Clemente Night at the ballpark.

Roberto also always remembered the fans that he had in Puerto Rico. He went home every year to play in the winter leagues. One winter he met and married Vera Christina Zabala. Soon Roberto and Vera had three sons, Roberto Jr., Luis, and Enrique. Vera went to Puerto Rico each time she had a baby because Roberto wanted all of his children to be born in Puerto Rico.

Most Valuable Player

Roberto was chosen as the National League's Most Valuable Player in 1966. Then in 1971, he got a hit just about 1 out of every 3 times that he was at bat. That is over 1/3 of the time—more than 33%! By 1966, Roberto had made 2,000 hits, and in 1972 he made hit number 3,000!

Roberto improved his hitting until he got a hit 1 out of every 3 times he was at bat.

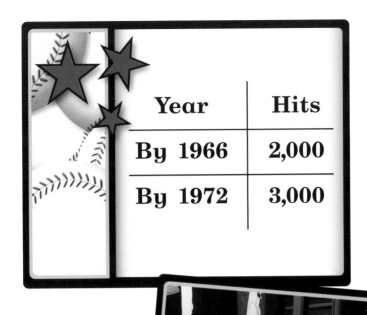

Year	Hits
By 1966	2,000
By 1972	3,000

Only 10 other players had ever reached 3,000 hits before.

Roberto the Hero

In December 1972, Roberto went home to Puerto Rico. He heard that Nicaragua had been hit by an earthquake. Thousands of people were hurt there. Because Roberto had traveled to Nicaragua and had many friends there, he decided to help.

The earthquake in Nicaragua caused many people to get hurt.

Roberto collected money, food, clothes, and medicine. He decided to take the supplies to Nicaragua himself. On New Year's Eve, he and four other men filled an old airplane with all of the items and left Puerto Rico. Shortly after the plane took off, it had engine trouble and crashed into the Atlantic Ocean. Roberto died trying to help others.

Divers looked for pieces from Roberto's plane crash.

After his death, Roberto was honored by others. In 1973 he was voted into the Baseball Hall of Fame, which is a group of only the best players. Usually a player is not given that honor until five years after his last ball game. Then the Pirates decided that no other Pirates' player would ever wear Roberto's number 21 on his uniform. It was a special way to honor and remember him.

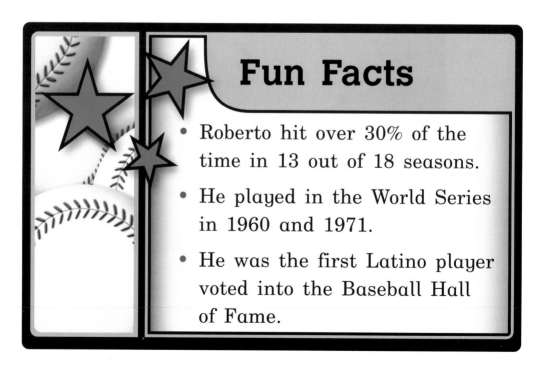

Fun Facts

- Roberto hit over 30% of the time in 13 out of 18 seasons.
- He played in the World Series in 1960 and 1971.
- He was the first Latino player voted into the Baseball Hall of Fame.

Roberto was a hero who wanted to help people. He had always dreamed of opening a place for poor children to play sports in Puerto Rico. After Roberto died, people gave money to help build a sports center for children. Since it has opened, over 100,000 children have learned about sports there.

Some people say that Roberto was the greatest player to play right field. Others say that nobody was a better baseball player than he. Most people agree that he was a great player and a good person.

A statue of Roberto stands at *Ciudad Deportivo,* or Sports City in Puerto Rico.

ROBERTO CLEMENTE EJEM

Roberto Clemente

(1934–1973)

1954
- Joins Dodgers' Montreal Royals
- Drafted by the Pirates

1934
Born in Carolina, Puerto Rico

1930   1940   1950

1952
- Joins Puerto Rican winter league
- Plays with Crabbers

1958
Hits 3 triples in 1 game to tie major league record

1964
Marries Vera Christina Zabala
in Puerto Rico

1961
Makes hit 1,000

1972
- Makes hit 3,000
- Dies in plane crash

1960   1970   1980

1966
- Makes hit 2,000
- First Puerto
  Rican to be
  named Most
  Valuable Player

1973
- First Latino player
  voted into the Baseball
  Hall of Fame
- Pirates decide that no
  other player will wear
  number 21

Index

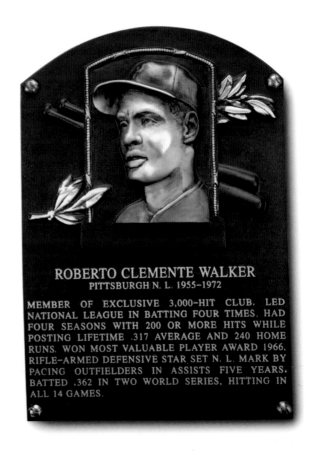

ROBERTO CLEMENTE WALKER
PITTSBURGH N. L. 1955–1972

MEMBER OF EXCLUSIVE 3,000-HIT CLUB. LED NATIONAL LEAGUE IN BATTING FOUR TIMES. HAD FOUR SEASONS WITH 200 OR MORE HITS WHILE POSTING LIFETIME .317 AVERAGE AND 240 HOME RUNS. WON MOST VALUABLE PLAYER AWARD 1966. RIFLE-ARMED DEFENSIVE STAR SET N. L. MARK BY PACING OUTFIELDERS IN ASSISTS FIVE YEARS. BATTED .362 IN TWO WORLD SERIES, HITTING IN ALL 14 GAMES.